INTRODUCING THE

BIRDS OF NORTH AMERICA

by David A. Hancock

BIRDS OF NORTH AMERICA SERIES is designed and produced by HANCOCK HOUSE PUBLISHERS. Regional editions of this book contain information on locating and identifying local bird species.

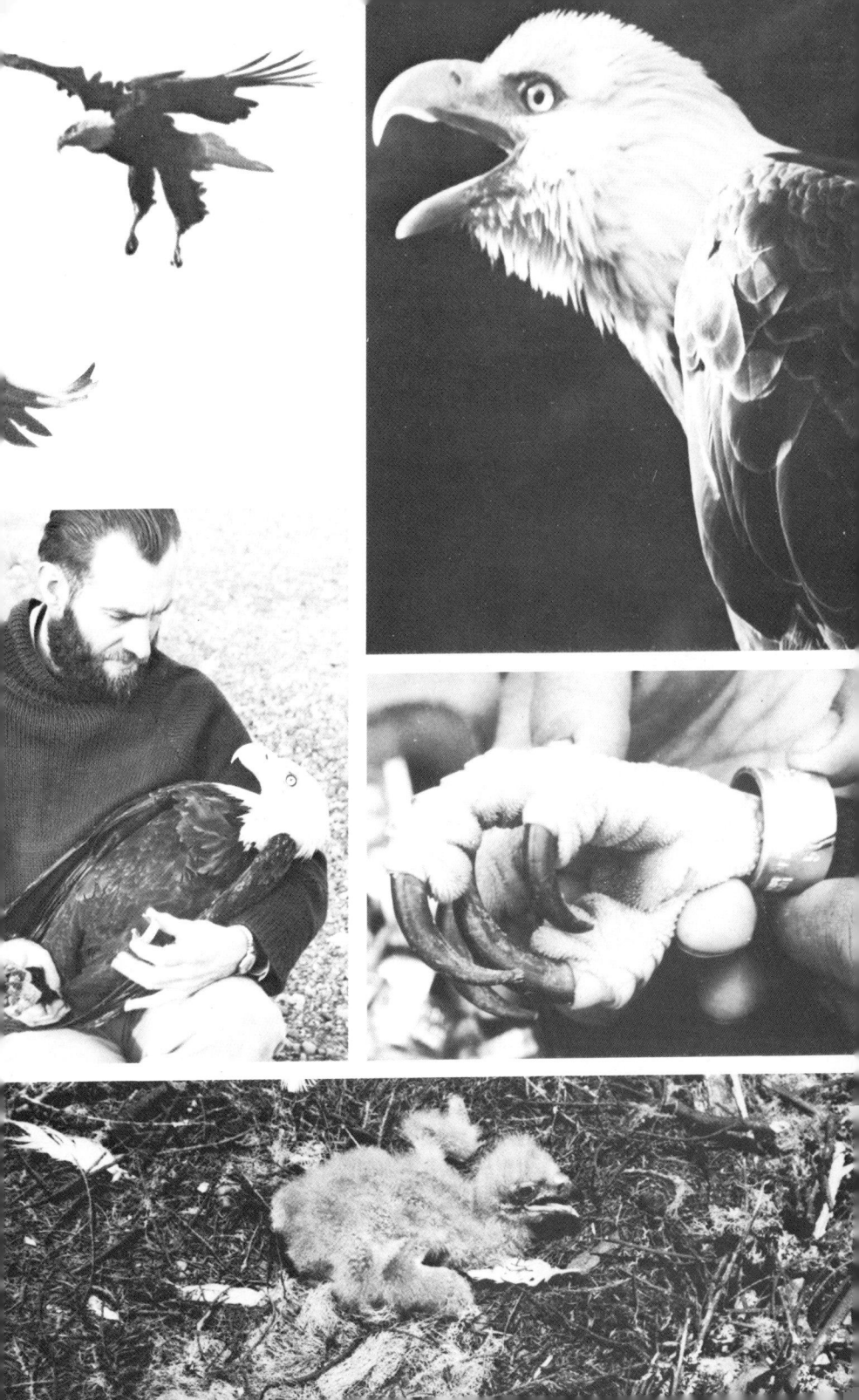

CONTENTS

PART 1 ABOUT BIRDS 6
- Distribution 6
- Classification 8
- Feathers and Flight 10
- Birds and Nests 13
- Migration 14
- Bird Society 15

PART 2 BIRD GROUPS 16
- Loons and Grebes 16
- Waterfowl 18
- Diurnal Predators 22
- Large Predators 23
- Falcons 23
- Eagles, Vultures, Ospreys, Hawks 25
- Lesser Predators 26
- Hawks and Kestrel 26
- Herons, Bitterns, Rails, and Coot 28
- Gulls, Terns, and Shorebirds 30
- Cormorant and Dove 32
- Nocturnal Predators 34
- Owls 34
- Nighthawk and Kingfisher 38
- Woodpecker 39
- Swallows 40
- Perching Birds 41

PART 3 BIRDWATCHING AND MORE 48
- Field Guides 48
- Bird Check List 50
- Binoculars 50
- Photography 50

Index to Species 53
Photograph Credits 53

Canadian Cataloguing in Publication Data

Hancock, David, 1938-
  Introducing the birds of North America

  (Birds of North America series)
  Includes index.
  ISBN 0-88839-220-6

  1. Birds - North America. I. Title.
  II. Series.

QL 681.H35 1989   598.297   C89-091221-1

Copyright © 1989 David Hancock   Printed in Hong Kong
Published simultaneously in Canada and the United States by

HANCOCK HOUSE PUBLISHERS LTD.
19313 Zero Ave., Surrey, B.C. V3S 5J9

HANCOCK HOUSE PUBLISHERS
1431 Harrison Ave., Blaine, WA 98230

PART 1
ABOUT BIRDS

DISTRIBUTION

WHAT IS A BIRD?

Birds are animals with feathers, descendants of scaly reptiles that ruled the earth hundreds of millions of years ago. Archaeopteryx, the earliest known fossil bird, appears to be nothing more than a lizard with feathers. Birds still have scales on their legs. Indeed, birds were around long before bird watchers came along to classify and enjoy them.

WHERE ARE BIRDS FOUND?

During this long period of geological time birds have evolved into many species of different shapes and sizes. They have specialized their tools for making a living and thereby adapted to many environments. Today more than 8000 bird species exist in the world. Except perhaps for the interior of Antarctica, birds occur in season over the entire earth. But some areas have poor bird fauna. These places include the polar regions and remote oceanic islands. Generally speaking, the further islands are from the continental land masses, the fewer birds they have, but all islands have some birds.

The largest variety of land birds inhabit temperate and sub-tropical savannah country, tropical semi-deserts and tropical forests. Two major factors control the distribution of birds. First, the number of plant species in the area affects the number of different habitats available for different birds to live in. Tropical forests with over 200 varieties of trees may house 500 bird species. Boreal forests of the north with only 10 or 12 tree species house fewer than 100 kinds of birds. The second factor is the ease by which a bird can find an area. A remote island will not often be found, particularly by birds that can't rest on water.

A Robin—our ubiquitous friend

Overleaf (p. 5): Bald Eagle scavenges dead, spawned-out salmon

B The Snowy Owl is an Arctic breeder who frequently is forced by weather and lack of food to seek southern winters

A The Golden Eagle was once found throughout the world. Now, in North America, the bird is commonly found only in the western mountains and the northern wilderness.

B This Tufted Puffin was caught with a faceful of fish. A western seabird, the puffin has Atlantic Coast cousins.

A Osprey

CLASSIFICATION

BY THEIR BEAKS AND FEET WE SHALL KNOW THEM

Ornithologists, scientists who study birds, recognize about 165 families of living birds. Birds are sorted into their family groups by checking the tools they use to make a living. A bird's tools include its feet and beak. Not many years ago it was said you could tell a man's occupation by looking at his hands. The parallel is not so simple today when even the laborer is influenced by television to keep his hands soft and his nails well manicured. Birds are more natural. By their beaks and feet we shall know them. The sparrows and grosbeaks have short, stout bills for crushing seeds, and feet adapted for hopping on the ground or from limb to limb. Waterfowl have webbed feet for swimming and wide bills for 'shoveling' up food. Grebes, loons, and herons have long, pointed bills for seizing or spearing fish. The flesh-eating hawks, falcons, and owls have strong talons for holding prey, and hooked beaks for tearing meat. The chisel beaks of the woodpeckers and sapsuckers enable them to split wood and bark to get at grubs and sap. The broad, gaping bill of the flycatchers, swallows, and nighthawks are ideal for scooping up insects on the wing. And so it goes; each family or species has its tools modified in a special way to facilitate its making a living.

B Peregrine Falcon adults feeding a thriving brood

A Ring-necked Pheasant

The digger	Ring-necked Pheasant
The prober	Greater Yellowlegs
The crusher	Evening Grosbeak
The chiseler	Yellow-bellied Sapsucker
The tearer	Sharp-shinned Hawk

B Greater Yellowlegs

C Nighthawk

D Evening Grosbeak

FEATHERS AND FLIGHT

Great Blue Heron

FLIGHT

Birds are the most mobile of earth's creatures. Wings come in many shapes and sizes and serve many purposes. Today, the Maribou Stork and the Wandering Albatross share the record for the longest wingspan—eleven feet. Bald and Golden Eagles sometimes attain a wingspan of seven feet; the Great Blue Heron (above), five-and-a-half feet. Pheasants and Ruffed Grouse have short, broad wings which allow them a quick burst of speed to escape predators, then a short glide to settle back to earth again. The swifts' long, narrow wings enable them to stay aloft for hours, and possibly even for days at a time. Many hawks and eagles have large, broad wings, permitting them to soar easily on warm, rising air bubbles over land. Falcons and other bird-catching hawks have much less wing surface area, allowing them to beat their wings much more rapidly for faster flight, but at the expense of soaring efficiency.

Flight serves to carry birds to food, away from predators, and seasonally on migration journeys. Flight also aids in courtship. The Peregrine Falcon and the Common Snipe perform aerial displays to attract their mates. The Ruffed Grouse, standing on a log, beats its wings to produce a drumming sound which declares ownership of its territory. Scoters, Common Murres, and penguins are capable of underwater flight.

SPEED OF FLIGHT	
Peregrine Falcon	
Diving	180 miles per hour
Level flight	60 miles per hour
Canada Goose	45 miles per hour
Mallard	55 miles per hour
Robin	30 miles per hour
Herring Gull	25 miles per hour
Starling	55 miles per hour

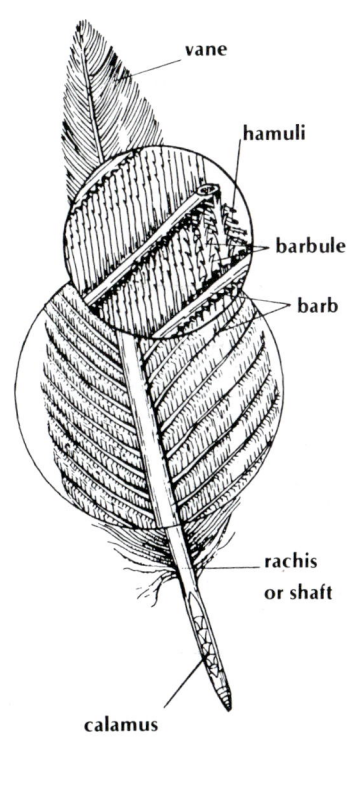

B Young Arctic Peregrine Falcon stops for rest on Eskimo fish-drying rack

FEATHERS

Feathers, collectively called plumage, give protection from the physical environment and are an aid to flight. Colored feathers or disruptive patterns can act as camouflage. A display of colorful feathers can help attract mates or repel competitors, and a brightly colored male bird can distract predators from the nesting female. The tail feathers of woodpeckers are stiff and act as a prop against the tree. The feathers on the face of barn owls are arranged in a disc, aiding in picking up and focusing minute sounds on the ear bones. Many waterfowl pluck out their undercoating of down feathers on the belly and use it to line their nests. The warm, bare belly skin helps to heat the eggs while the down in the nest prevents the loss of heat to the cold outside air.

A   Semi-palmated Plover

B   Young Bald Eagles, nearly fledged

The Semi-palmated Plover (above) nests in a shallow scraping on a bare ground while the Bald Eagles (below) build an elaborate nest 5-12 feet across in a secluded tree.

BIRDS AND NESTS

In size, North America's birds range from the Calliope Hummingbird, weighing only an eighth of an ounce, to the 38-pound Trumpeter Swan. Bald and Golden Eagles are often thought to be much heavier than they really are. The males weigh between 5 and 7 pounds, the females between 8 and 12 pounds.

THE BIG AND THE SMALL

Since they can lift and carry only about one-quarter of their weight, there is little truth in the old wives' tales about eagles carrying off lambs and calves—that is, unless you have a herd of 2-pound cows! The heaviest birds in the world are the Ostrich and the Emu, which have sacrificed their ability to fly.

A   Trumpeter Swans

B   Calliope Hummingbird

NESTS

Bird nests vary greatly in size and structure. Cowbirds and cuckoos avoid the chores of nest building and parenthood altogether, by laying their eggs in someone else's nest. The foster parent then does all the work. Oystercatchers, Nighthawks, and Peregrine Falcons make no nest, or lay their eggs in a shallow scraping in the gravel.

Woodpeckers chisel out nest cavities in trees, which are in turn used by an assortment of other birds—bluebirds, Tree Swallows, Wood Ducks, and Starlings. Warblers and vireos make elaborate nests lined with down, hair, the gossamer of willows, and often camouflaged with lichens.

The function of a nest is to offer protection for the eggs and the developing young. Tufted Puffins, which nest in deep burrows on remote islands and spend most of their life out on the open ocean where there are few predators, get by with laying just one egg. The Ruffed Grouse and the Pheasant, which nest on exposed ground and whose eggs are eaten by many predators—snakes, skunks, and man—lay many eggs. And, as with most ground-nesting birds, the young are precocial. That is, they are able to get up and move around to feed and avoid enemies as soon as they hatch. In contrast, the young Bald Eagle doesn't leave the nest until it is fully grown and able to fly—at the age of 10 $\frac{1}{2}$ weeks.

MIGRATION

A   Snow Geese

Migration is any regular movement between two areas brought about by changes in environmental conditions. In North America, seasonal migrations usually follow a north and south direction. Some birds perform seasonal migrations even within the tropics. Others are wanderers, moving with the wet and dry seasons which determine their food supplies.

There is no one answer to account for the migration of birds. Nature, however, abhors a vacuum. In summer, vast areas of the frozen north thaw, and temporarily become suitable homes for birds. Insects, seeds, and other foods become abundant, and birds, because they are mobile, move in. Only a few species, such as the Gyr Falcon and its prey, the ptarmigan, are adapted to the rigors of the northern winters. The Arctic Tern, for example, may travel 30,000 miles over North and South America to Africa, and back to the north to breed. Also, there are daily migrations—to and from feeding areas and roosts.

Generally speaking, large birds migrate by day; smaller ones move by night, when they can avoid predators. Birds such as cranes and hawks fly by day to take advantage of the rising hot air bubbles. By circling over a rising air mass, they gain height, then glide for miles to the next thermal. In mountainous country, there are also local, altitudinal migrations. During the spring melt, birds move from their winter habitat in the valleys to higher elevations as nesting sites and food become available.

B   Flock of Sanderlings

B Arctic Terns

BIRD SOCIETY

Most birds are sociable, at least seasonally, though some hawks, owls, and woodpeckers live singly, except during breeding season. Robins, ducks, and sandpipers gather in flocks during migration but form into pairs for the breeding season when they are intolerant of others of their own kind and sex. Gulls and sea birds, on the other hand, form into loosely associated groups only during the winter; in summer, they congregate into highly organized colonies to breed. These different social systems aid in survival.

Sea birds spend most of the year widely dispersed over the open oceans, but for nesting require isolated islands free of land predators. These specialized requirements force sea birds to congregate on a few suitable islands, making sociability a necessity. Although colony nesting birds often appear to nest without any order, there is, in fact, a minimum distance of a foot or so between each nest. This is the pecking reach of each bird and it assures some privacy and space to each pair.

In contrast, such birds as Song Sparrows and Cooper's Hawks defend considerably larger territories. This ensures that a minimal food supply is exclusively theirs. The gathering of birds into colonies makes it easier for them to find mates, coordinate their breeding activities, and defend their nests. A disadvantage is the disturbance of many birds at one time by pleasure boaters and vandals.

PART 2   BIRD GROUPS

LOONS AND GREBES

Loons sit low in the water, propel themselves underwater with webbed feet to catch fish, and never emerge onto land except to nest. The Common Loon is famed for its yodel-like laugh.

Grebes are weak-flying, tailless water birds with lobed toes.

A   The eggs

B   The first chick

C   The departure

Pied-billed Grebe

A   Horned Grebe

17

B   Common Loon

A   Mallard with young   18

WATERFOWL

DUCKS, GEESE, AND SWANS

Scientists have counted 148 kinds of waterfowl around the world. Some 63 species live in North America. All members of this order are adapted for life in the water. They have webbing between their 3 front toes, and flattened bills with tooth-like edges that act as strainers. Most species are strong fliers, undertaking long migration flights between breeding areas in the north and wintering areas in the south. The young are down-covered and can walk and swim a few hours after hatching.

B   Mute Swan

Canada Goose

20

A Greater Scaup (female)

B Wood Duck

C Gadwall

D American Widgeon

E Pintail   Ring-necked Pheasant

A Immature Peregrine Falcon

B Arctic Peregrine Falcons at eyrie

DIURNAL PREDATORS

LARGE PREDATORS:
FALCONS

All birds, for at least part of their lives, live on other animals and are, therefore, predators. Usually, however, predators are considered as either diurnal—the daytime hunters such as the hawks, falcons, and eagles—or nocturnal—the night-time hunters such as owls. The diurnal hunters are some of the most colorful, spectacular, and yet least understood of any birds. The beautiful Peregrine Falcon is an endangered species because it has been unjustly shot, driven from its breeding grounds by encroaching human activities, and had its food (and consequently itself) poisoned by pesticides.

Peregrine Falcon and day-old chick

A   Adult Bald Eagle   24   B   Red-tailed Hawk

A   Osprey

B   Immature Goshawk

EAGLES, VULTURES, OSPREYS, AND HAWKS

Predator size is definitely not the only criterion in determining prey size. Our largest eagle, the Bald Eagle, feeds primarily on small fish or carcasses of dead animals. The Turkey Vulture feeds exclusively on carrion.

The smaller, 8-12 pound Golden Eagle, however, is an active predator that can kill jackrabbits, marmots, and even foxes.

The Osprey has scaly toes and sharp talons especially suited for catching and holding fish.

The Red-tailed Hawk, along with the other broad-winged soaring hawks, are often unjustly blamed for raiding barnyards. These soaring hawks are often seen around farms, hunting their main prey of mice, rats, snakes, and insects.

C   Golden Eagle

D   Turkey Vulture

LESSER PREDATORS:

HAWKS AND KESTREL

In most birds of prey, the male and female look alike, though the females are always larger. The Sharp-shinned Hawk, Cooper, and Merlin are strictly bird-catching hawks. They occasionally become a nuisance around bird feeders because the unnatural concentration of prey around feeders is a natural attraction to the predator. If plenty of brush cover is provided, however, the feeding birds will not be unfairly exposed to the hunters. The delicately built Marsh Hawk and Kestrel are rodent and insect feeders.

A   Rough-legged Hawk

B   Rough-Legged Hawk

A   Killdeer   31   B   Black-bellied Plover

A Double-crested Cormorants   32

CORMORANT AND DOVE

B Mourning Dove

OWLS

Young Saw-whet Owl with mouse

A Great Horned Owl in nest

NOCTURNAL PREDATORS

THE OWLS

No group of birds more elicits a feeling of comradeship, empathy, or respect than the owls. Their wise expression comes from the fact that their eyes are fixed in their sockets. The owl must turn its head to focus on an object, thus giving the appearance of 100 percent attention and concentration. All owls fly silently to aid in hearing their prey and in approaching it. The leading edges of their flight feathers are supple and soft and so they make no noise rubbing together or against the air.

Great Horned Owl

B Young Great Horned Owls

A   Snowy Owl

B   Long-eared Owl

The Horned Owl, or Tiger of the Woods (previous 2 pages), and his smaller cousin the Screech Owl, nest very successfully around farms or in towns. Most owls eat mice, rats, and rabbits, though many of the smaller owls also consume great quantities of insects. Generally nocturnal in habit, the Snowy Owl of the north and the local Short-eared Owl do considerable hunting by daylight or at dusk.

D   Barred Owl

C   Screech Owl at nest box

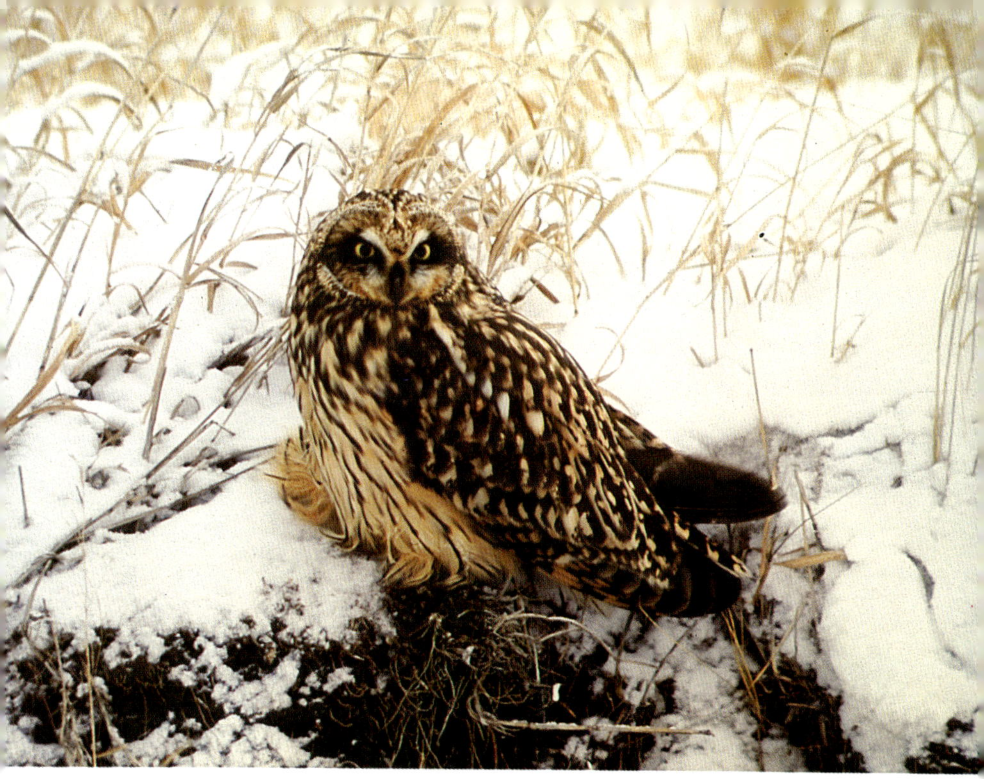

A   Short-eared Owl

B   Young Saw-whet Owls

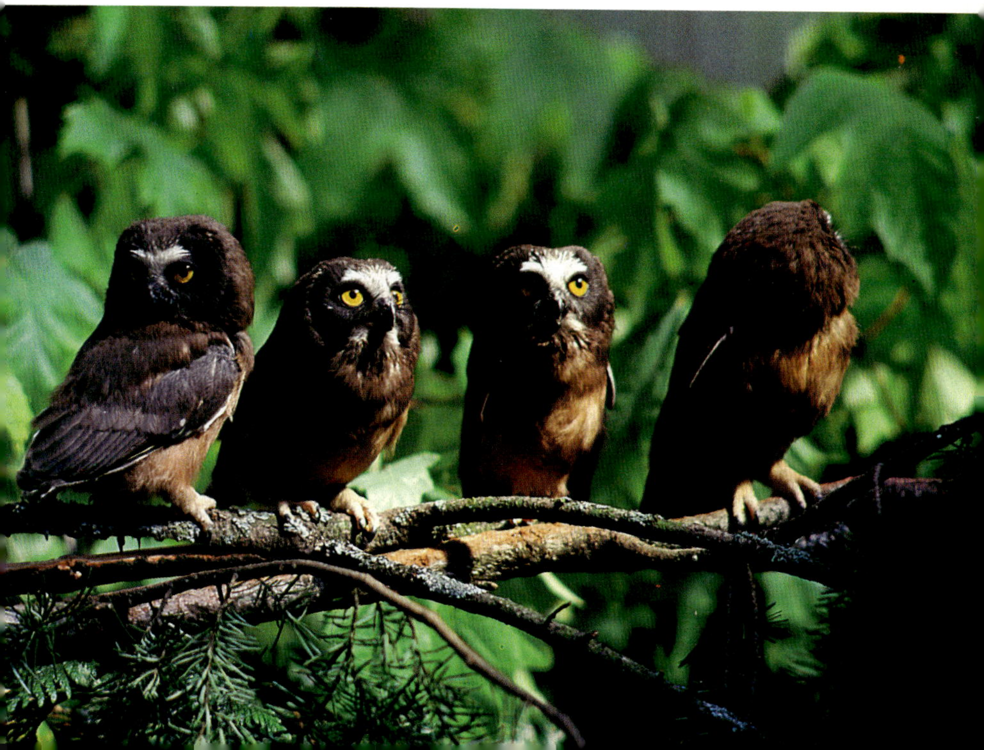

NIGHTHAWK AND KINGFISHER

A Nighthawk

B Young Belted Kingfishers

WOODPECKER

Yellow-bellied Sapsucker

A Barn Swallows

SWALLOWS

Elegant, beneficial, graceful, bold, or beautiful—few birds more qualify for compliments than the diminutive swallows.

All have long, pointed wings, usually a forked or notched tail, small weak feet, and a wide, gaping bill for snatching up insects on the wing.

The group is adapted to living under many circumstances, nesting in tree holes, rock cavities, or with a mud nest stuck to cliffs or buildings.

B Male Tree Swallow

C Cliff Swallows

A Loggerhead Shrike

PERCHING BIRDS

These two and the next six pages deal with the perching birds, or passerines. They constitute by far the largest and most diverse group of birds and present the greatest challenge for identification.

B Blue Jay

C Raven

A Cedar Waxwings   42
              C Eastern
                 Kingbird
B White-breasted Nuthatch

A House Wren

B Red-eyed Vireo

A Yellow Warbler, male and female with young

B Least Flycatcher

A   Horned Lark

B   Pine Grosbeak (male)

C   Evening Grosbeak (female)

A American Goldfinch

B White-crowned Sparrow   **C** Slate-colored Junco

A   Purple Finch

B   Grasshopper Sparrow

C   Fox Sparrow

PART 3 **BIRD WATCHING AND MORE**

Bird watching is a disease. It can strike rapidly and without regard to age or sex. Accordingly to recent surveys, there are more than 20 million bird watchers in North America—truly a disease of epidemic proportions! But why? The answer is simple. Birds are everywhere, from the back yard to wilderness areas of every continent. Their diversity of size, shape, color, and behavior offer exciting challenges for indoor or outdoor recreation. Bird watching can be a private interlude in the day, a social gathering, a science, or a business through the sale of your stories or photographs of birds.

Not all bird photography requires long waits in blinds. For example, some owls, such as this Saw-whet Owl, can be approached quite closely in the daytime for a close-up portrait. While the owls can see perfectly well in daylight, they often prefer to sit tight rather than fly and risk the wrath of crows.

Mallard with brood

▲ Saw-whet Owl

In fact, bird watching is big business. More books are devoted to the birds than to any other field of natural history. Hundreds of millions of dollars are spent annually on automobiles, motels, and travel tours directly by people pursuing birds. Camera, binocular, telescope, and tape recorder sales to birders contribute even more. And the manufacture of bird feeders and the sale of bird food supports thousands of persons.

Good binoculars and an easy-to-use field guide are the essential tools for the bird watcher. The bird watcher's disease, however, can cause fevered and irrational behavior; I suspect this is the reason so many birders stumble into the woods armed with extra check lists, cameras with multiple lenses, and tape recorders equipped with parabolic reflectors. Here, then, is a practical introduction to bird-watching hardware.

FIELD GUIDES

A good field guide contains clear illustrations of the birds for easy identification, a range map to quickly tell when and where a bird is likely to be found, and a brief description of the bird's behavior, habitat, and easily identifiable characteristics. Nothing more need be said than GET:

Birds of North America by National Geographic Society. Soft Cover. The best book but not readily available.

Birds of North America by Robbins, Bruun, Zim, and Singer. Golden Press. Hard or soft bound.

BIRD CHECK LISTS

Check lists are simply a local (city) or regional compilation of all birds found in the area concerned (see page 66). They are made of stiff card for carrying in the pocket or field guide. They usually state whether a bird is commonly or rarely seen, and at what season. Most Natural History clubs make these available to visiting birders, free or for about 25 cents each. The cards make it easy to record the day's sightings, and to form a permanent record. Get them for the areas you visit. Keep notes on your sitings—over the years they are not just interesting for comparison but can be of great value to biologists studying population changes.

BINOCULARS

These come in a wide range of quality, price, and power. Don't get a magnification of more than 6, 7, or 8 power. It's impossible to hold more powerful ones steady under perfect conditions, let alone after running 100 yards through the woods after a 'new bird.' For the untried beginner, many excellent, yet heavier pairs, can be purchased for $30 to $60. Avoid the $200 to $300 pairs. Recent advances in optics and lightweight bodies such as the Nikon or Bushnell ultra-compact prism binoculars bring quality, durability, and lightness for $70 to $100.

PHOTOGRAPHY

Without proper care, bird photography can become the most malignant outgrowth of birding, draining dollars, time, and the spouse's patience. On the other hand, the ultimate challenge in seeing a new bird or its exciting behavior is to record it on film for later reference, or for friends, business, or science. The photographs in this book come almost exclusively from amateur birder-naturalists. And why not make an enjoyable hobby pay its way?

There are two important features in bird photography. First, you must know the habits of your subjects. That is, know where to go to look for them and be able to predict their behavior patterns and understand their tolerances to your disturbance. Once you have found out where a bird is likely to appear, then only patient waiting (often from the seclusion of a blind) is required to capture exciting moments on film. That is, provided you thoroughly understand the second important feature of photography—the operation of your camera and film.

There are dozens of good camera makes and models highly suitable for bird photography. Unfortunately, many camera stores give advice dependent

Photography Blind

Great Horned Owl

upon the availability of stock and the discount that they make on selling. Here are some specifications that suit this photographer.

First, get a reflex camera—where you look through the lens to see exactly what is being photographed and whether it is in focus. Second, the 35 mm format is most flexible for optional lenses and attachments, is lightweight and easy to carry, is simple and quick to use, and is economical to keep fed with film.

Two basic lenses will take 99 percent of your pictures. First is a macro zoom lens with a focal length range of about 28-100 mm. The macro lens permits pictures to be taken within one foot. This is particularly important if you are out birding and want a close-up of a bee, flower, or nest. Oh, you're not interested in insects and flowers? Well, the birds are, and most birders quickly develop an appreciation of all nature.

The second lens I recommend is a telephoto of moderate length—150 to 200 mm. This can be hand held at 125th of a second to give flexibility for 'opportunistic' photography. That is, getting a picture whenever you can. This is opposed to setting up the equipment in a blind, possibly with strobe lights and a super abundance of patience. A large telephoto of 400 to 500 mm is a seldom-used frill that can come much, much later.

In wildlife photography it is often desirable to change lenses quickly to get a shot of a fleeing subject. Here, a bayonet mount on the lense is helpful. Also, go the few extra dollars and get a through-the-lens meter, or even a fully automatic camera. Today the new computerized cameras even come to the aid of those who find focusing difficult. For $500 you can get a new outfit with the two lenses, and the accommodating shop clerk will be pleased to throw in a free roll of film, knowing he has another birder hooked.

Overleaf—Adult Bald Eagle